meditations
to ease, calm & inspire

A COLLECTION TO ACTIVATE
YOUR MIND AND SOUL

BY SUSAN LOWENTHAL AXELROD

**Meditations to Ease, Calm and Inspire:
A Collection to Activate Your Mind and Soul**

ISBN: 978-0-578-53297-4

First Edition - June 2019

Copyright © 2019 by Susan Lowenthal Axelrod

All rights reserved. No part of this book may be reproduced in any form without written permission from the copyright holder.

Published by JGU Press. Printed in the USA.

Design & Layout by Carasmatic Design - www.CarasmaticDesign.com

CONTENTS

Preface...6

Introduction: Quieting Your Mind................................8

1. On Clearing...10

2. Your Job is to Be..15

3. Hidden Blessings...19

4. The Divine Message Within...................................23

5. On Feeling Certain...27

6. Your Journey to Prosperous Abundance.........31

7. On Flowing Milk..36

8. A Journey of Loving & Cleansing Your Body..40

9. Finding Your Inner Strength..................................46

10. What do I Know?..51

11. Too Much...56

12. B.O.A.T. Meditation to Find the Calm Within..60

13. I Help Heal...64

14. On Comparison..67

15. In Healing for All Who Have Said "Me, Too"..73

16. Stay on the Path...77

17. There is Light...81

18. What's it Going to Take?......................................84

Conclusion: Feeling Clear and Open: What's Next?..88

PREFACE

For a long time, I lived in a place that might be called tormented, certainly anxious. My mind was constantly filled, cluttered, chaotic. This did not go well for me. I ended up having a break that landed me in bed for a week or more, anxious, depressed and unable to function well. It was my lowest point and finally activated a deep yearning: *I want to feel better than this.*

I learned that this was a first step into the *journey of self*, wanting to feel better than your current state. *Your soul always wants to feel better; that's all, just better.* In order to do that, she needs clearing, quiet, intention, commitment and most importantly, a deep desire. I worked at all of these things.

I began to listen to and learn from others, others who had been on their soul journey for decades. Then, I processed by speaking about and sharing what I learned. To my surprise, I found myself opening up and *feeling* deeply. I had not realized that my feelings were suppressed. I cried a lot. I learned that these tears were my soul showing herself.

As I was opening to my own soul journey, I shared my experiences more and I grew further still. I discovered that I had Intuition (you do, too, if you open to it). And I opened more. I started coaching and during sessions with clients, custom Affirmations came forth. And I opened more. Finally, Meditations came forth and people told me they were helpful. With the positive feedback I have received from people who have heard my meditations, I decided to create this small book to help anyone who might need support to clear their own mind and find their own ease.

INTRODUCTION

Quieting Your Mind

Dear Reader,

Once upon a time...I was a stressed and distressed Type-A, mocking those who talked about the soul, the spirit, God and anything related to meditation, mindfulness, being present or even being happy [c'mon now, was I the only one not tuned in?].

I did meet and marry a handsome prince, but that has nothing to do with my soul-journey story, except inasmuch as he has lovingly supported me along the way. As have many others, but I did the work. The work of moving up the *better-feeling scale*. From feeling horrible to not horrible, from not horrible to acceptable, from acceptable to OK! I celebrated when I got to OK! Small victories, I did not need things to be perfect, 'OK' was good enough. But, in the end, I went from getting 'ok' with myself, to feeling so much better about my life and further still to find a place of ease and calm in my soul and quiet in my mind [my old Type-A self does still visit sometimes, just to keep-it-real, I guess!].

Before I got so 'zen,' I used to ask myself frantically: What is happening to me? Where on earth did these guided meditations in me come from? Where is the person who used to mock meditation? The person who used to declare with conviction, "I can't meditate," or "I can't clear my mind."

I used to ask myself these questions, in wonder. And I resisted the idea that something I wrote could have a place in the world to help others find some ease, "I'm no yogi, I'm just a regular person." I used to resist the idea that I could create something that would uplift someone else's spirit.

Turns out, I could.

I hope these meditations serve you on your own journey to a calm and confident-life.

Wishing you all the best always,

Susan

NOTE: I learned a little secret that I am happy to share with you. If you voice-dictate the guided meditations and listen to them in your own voice, there is exponential soul-connection! It becomes a truly self-guided journey. If, however, you are not inclined to voice record every meditation, then you will find them all available on my website at www.whatwillyourlegacybe.com/confident-life-marketplace.

ON CLEARING

If you struggle to find that space to clear your mind and get quiet inside, this meditation will serve you. Getting clear and quiet will reveal the hidden blessings in your life.

It's okay to ask why. Why is it important to clear my mind, what does that do for me, how does it serve me? Why is it important to clear my mind?

Let's explore this, let's see if we can discover the answer. But before we do let's take a breath, deep breath in and long breath out. And another, deep breath in, and long breath out.

Why is it important to clear my mind? Take a moment now to consider what is on your mind. What is it that you are thinking about this moment, what are you thinking about from an hour ago, from your day, from your night, from the week that you have had, from the year that you have had, what is it that is on your mind?

When you take time to consider and reflect, when you take time to go in and navigate through and around the masses of thoughts that reside in your mind, you will become aware of how much is there. For some it is more obvious, always filled, always pressing, creating tension, stress, overwhelm and then anxiety. Thoughts constantly running through your mind racing to beat out each other to take the place of central focus. But alas, there is no winner in that race because of the number of entrants. How many? Too many to even number, crowded, bumping into each other, knocking each other out of the way to try to get ahead. So many thoughts, how many? Too many to count.

Is this true for you? Can you feel the breathlessness of the race, each runner straining to get ahead, each thought straining to get noticed?

Or, is your mind dark, devoid, murky in the swamp of mire that drains your energy and forward motion? In this place, you may not be able to come up with thoughts, but they are there, hidden underneath the weeds that have grown so thick that the thoughts get entwined in a way that is dank, not clear.

What does a clear mind feel like? It feels comfortable and calm, light and airy. It feels overtly upbeat and steadfastly settled. The heart quiets down, the soul relaxed.

What does a clear mind feel like?

Why is it important to clear your mind? To give your body a break, to support your soul, to create the type of vibration that supports you and the world. Permit your mind to support yourself, to reduce angst and you will be able to lift up yourself and from there uplift others, and from the uplifting *it is so*, that you can clearly realize your gifts, your impact, the impact that is intended for you to make. *It is so* that you can clearly see the way, the path for you to walk, to feel alive. To awaken the deadened senses that are stymied from the entanglement of thoughts and feelings that have grown over and through the beauty of the garden in you.

Why is it important that you clear your mind? When you sit for a moment in clarity the weeds fall away, there is a clearing for you to discover yourself again, there is a place for your soul to dwell.

Do you have to? Do you have to clear your mind? No, no you don't. You are fine just as you are. However, if you have the desire to give your mind, body and soul a break, to explore the beauty in you, to know your gifts, to know your purpose then try using your breath. Try simply to be, allow yourself to clear, clear, clear and clear some more until you feel that settled feeling. The racing thoughts slow, they slow some more, they are walking now comfortably, calmly slowing further still. You can feel your heart slowing as each one of the thoughts slows further still.

And now, one by one they drop away, drop away, drop away. One by one they settle down; they sit and stay. Perfectly calm, no longer vibrating just fading, fading, fading.

And now, you can begin to feel what 'Clear' feels like, you can begin to feel that lighter airier feeling; clarity, knowing that you are okay, that your mind is just clearing, clearing, clearing.

Your body already feeling more buoyant, light as a feather. This is what it feels like to have your mind clear. This is why it is important to clear your mind. Clarity, for you to be able to think in the positive way you want, to feel good, to feel okay. To feel that all is well and that now you can be who you want to be and live how you want to live, in your control, in your control, in your control.

Take a breath now, and blow it out. And another, deep breath in and long breath out.

Why is it important to clear your mind? Your clear mind serves you to be who you want to be and to live the life you want. The power is in you.

reflections

2

YOUR JOB IS TO BE

When you need to calm your inner angst and that feeling of having to do everything, all the time, and especially the feeling of 'must do it now.' Use this meditation to remember that the highest good is just to be.

We are here, just here, in this moment. That is all.

We are here, just here, in this moment.

Take a breath, deep breath in and long breath out. Take another breath now, deep breath in, all the way in, and let it out.

Take this moment now, to clear your mind. Clear your mind of the cluttered thoughts, that reside there. Tripping and traipsing through the pathways of your mind, entangled with each other. Visualize your

We are here, just here, in this moment.

own hands, fingers combing combing combing through the thoughts, bringing them into orderly rows that you can catalog and file. All the memories, all the activities, all the worries sitting orderly, catalogued in an organized way. For you, it may look like files, maybe a spreadsheet, or a matrix, use your inner manager to bring order to the entangled mass of thoughts that clog your mind. Fingers combing, combing, combing; can you see them untangling, can you see the order, can you allow your mind now to clear?

Take this moment now to clear your body of the conflicted feelings that are found within.

Another jumbled entangled mass but this time it is so many feelings that course through your body. The entanglement showing itself as sadness, as fear, or other negative emotions that cloud your consciousness. Take a breath now, and visualize your hands soothing, soothing, soothing the emotions; soothing, soothing, soothing the feelings. Feel them, settling, settling. Take another breath now. The feelings are still there, each one valid, but each one now in its place, settled and calm. Honor every feeling as it does serve a purpose in you.

But for now, we are here, just here, in this moment. Thoughts in order, feelings settled. We are here, just here, we are okay.

This is the natural state of being, we are human beings. This is what it feels like to be, just to be. No worries, no anxiety, settled feelings. We are here, just here, in this moment. That is all. For just this moment, this is all there is; this is now and this is eternity. This very moment is all there is. For just this moment, we are here, just here, now. When I am okay in this moment, then I start the next moment from okay. When I start the next moment as okay, then the next moment after that starts from okay. And so on and so on. The same holds true for sad. When I start this moment as sad, then the next moment after that starts from sad. When I start the next moment from sad, then the moment after that starts from sad. Do you see? Do you see what we do? It is within our power to be okay in this moment, by your breath, through your desire, it is in your control.

How, you wonder? You choose. You simply choose to be okay in this moment, to just be in this moment. You simply choose. You can! It is! It is in your control, the thoughts you think, the feelings you feel in this moment, you choose.

We are here, just here, in this moment. That is all. Your job is to be.

reflections

3

HIDDEN BLESSINGS

There are a myriad of blessings hidden in our lives every minute of every day if you see them. Open to the possibility that they are there, waiting for you to discover.

Take a moment to shut your eyes, stretch your shoulders, gently move your head from side to side and stretch your neck. Now breathe, deep breath in and long breath out. And breathe again.

What if....

What if the next time you were in a dark place, you remembered that there are Hidden Blessings there?

What if, instead of spiraling downward into any negative emotion, you caught yourself, you loved yourself and you breathed. Take a deep breath in now and a long breath out.

In spite of the twists and turns, can you see the good?

What if you remind yourself that all things that happen have reason. And just know that when things go wrong, as they sometimes will, it helps to know about the secret of Hidden Blessings.

Think back to a time in your life when something went very wrong, when you were in that place of difficulty, that you thought you might never leave. Your thoughts were dark, the world seemed dark and everything seemed affected by that darkness. Feel that difficulty now, and breathe. Breathe in, breathe out.

Now, fast forward only a short period of time. It may have been minutes, it may have been days, it may have taken months or even years and yet here you are today, in the light. How did you get from that time to this? The answer is Hidden Blessings.

It may seem hard to believe that there were blessings in the difficulty, but they were there. We know they were there, because we are here today.

It is a blessing to realize that every twist and turn in life is simply part of the journey you are on; it is not the end, it is never the end, until your body returns to dust. And even then, the soul still continues on its journey, only your body is gone.

It is a blessing to see life this way! If you do, when you are in the darkness, you can remember and look for the Blessings. You can breathe, and open your eyes and see the possibility of better outcomes. You can remember other difficult times that taught you lessons that later enriched your life.

If you realize this, then the next time you come to a dark place, you can remember **that**; look and see what good ended up coming out of the bad.

In spite of the twists and turns, can you see the good? Can you see the eventual light, the direction that you might not have gone in, but for a moment of darkness? Take a breath now, deep breath in and long breath out.

If you can see or know this, you can feel grateful, even for the dark moments. They serve to help the light-moments shine brightly by contrast.

Now, breathe again, deep breath in and long breath out.

Remember your Hidden Blessings.

reflections

THE DIVINE MESSAGE WITHIN

Did you know that you have a divine message within you? It is a message that was born with you that you are intended to find, to know and to share. This meditation supports the exploration of your divine message.

I invite you to contemplate your divine message within.

Close your eyes. Take a moment to breathe; deep breath in and long breath out.

Clear away the thoughts of the day, of concern, of anything other than the divine inspiration that is your soul's yearning to share. Breathe again. Deep breath in and long breath out. Look for the quiet, find the calm… see the space of knowing your truth. Listen, what do you hear?

A whisper, inspiring you. Don't worry about whether or not you can hear it clearly, precisely,

Listen, what do you hear?

plainly; listen for the suggestion, the idea of what's in you, of what the world is waiting to hear. Breathe again. Relax your shoulders.

Listen now.

It may be a mere word, a thought, a wisp of an impression; or it may be loud and strong and clear. Either way, keep listening. Later, when you are done with this meditation, you can write, write, write. But for now, stay quiet inside and listen, listen, listen.

What do you hear?

While you are quiet now, ask questions. What is my purpose? What is the message in me to share with the world? Who is waiting to hear it? What are the words that are intended to come together? Where will I speak? How will I get there? These questions will spark your inner dialogue, don't worry about speaking in public. Sharing your message with a single soul is as powerful as sharing it with an audience of hundreds.

Thank God or your Universal Source for the gleaning, commit to coming back to this space every now and then to listen again, to learn more, to grow and know of the impact you are intended to make.

Breathe now, and offer a silent blessing to that sacred space, that sacred voice that is uniquely yours. You can go there whenever you want, whenever you need quiet.

When you're ready, open your eyes, gently roll your shoulders and breathe.

reflections

5

ON FEELING CERTAIN

If you feel constantly in doubt or unsure of your place, your space, your words, or your thoughts, this meditation will serve.

How do I know? How can I be sure?

Start with your breath. Take a deep breath in and long breath out.

Open your mind to the energy of being certain, breathe again, deep breath in and long breath out. Expel all the air from your body. Breathe again.

Sit up straight, gently stretch your shoulders back, roll them to the front. Gently stretch your neck to the right, to the left, gently up, gently down. Breathe again and feel the calm settle over you like a silken layer, soft to the touch, but strong as the unerringly woven threads and with the beauty of a jewel's deep hue.

Look for the light in your mind.

Know that energy -like your blood- is flowing freely throughout your body. This energy will serve you as you begin to open to receiving certainty.

Ask the question: Is this right? Is it wrong?

Look for the light in your mind. Do you see it? If you search, you will find...a small clear space...a point of light. It is clear, it is bright, it is sure. That is your knowing. This is right.

Now, turn away from the light for a moment...do you suddenly feel the obscurity? It is dark, the footing is unsure; it may seem too cold, too hot, murky or muddled. Can you feel that feeling...the feeling of not being certain? Check in with your body, how does it feel now? Start with your crown and scan down to your toes. Stop along the way at the points of energy as they present themselves, perhaps in the organs, perhaps in the muscles, perhaps in the tissue, honor any point of doubt. Turn towards it, face it squarely and see that it is just a mist, it dissipates with a single energetic turn, back to the point of light.

Back to the light, it is clear, it is bright it is sure; your knowing.

It is not arrogant to know...Knowing *can* be steeped in arrogance: I'm 'better than' because I know or, it can be imbued with calm-I'm confident because I know.

...What do I know? Do I know everything? Or, do I know myself-my humility, suffused with my purpose?

What 'I know' is a feeling, that I am on the right track, that I am headed in the right direction, that my purpose in this moment is clear. I, I, I. Yes, you. You, made in G-d's image, not perfection, but omniscient, sure. Sure, that in this moment, your knowing leads you, through this one step, this one thought, confidently on the way to the next. And the next.

I am sure.

Take a breath now, do a body scan again, check in with your body, how does it feel now? Start with your toes, grounded in your new certainty, move all the way up to your crown, the white light of knowing bursting forth. Breathe again, deep breath in and long breath out. I am Sure.

reflections

6

YOUR JOURNEY TO PROSPEROUS ABUNDANCE

Prosperity can come in the form of money, but your prosperous abundance will grow manifold if you realize that prosperity comes to you in the form of blessings. Then, you can get clear on seeing money in the light and as the sea in which you swim, and you will realize exponential returns!

Open up to the world of abundance, of prosperity. Close your eyes, take a moment to stretch your shoulders and your neck, breathe gently, in and out, put your feet on the floor, feel them firmly planted. Take another breath, deep breath in, long breath out.

It only takes a moment to break through the protective shield of scarcity that surrounds us. That feeling of 'there's never enough,' or 'I wish I had,' or 'if only.' It's comfortable; it's familiar, it's like a warm

Prosperous abundance is light in the form of love.

shroud that covers you, you hold it closely around your body. Except that shroud is suffocating you. Feel that now, there's a shortness of breath in the feeling of not enough.

Now, open up to the world of abundance, of prosperity; to the world of *there is enough*. Take a deep breath in and long breath out. And again, a deep breath in and long breath out

Feel yourself in this clear breathing space. Now, think of the light above your head that you imagine when you think of wealth, prosperity, abundance and all things plentiful. When you think of these concepts, no doubt, you see them bathed in light.

Before we go on, I want to invite you to breathe good into that light that you see with your mind. Breathe the good from your heart, the good from your soul into that light. Sometimes, that light can blind. Take a moment now to breathe, and breathe again.

Now that there is good in the light of prosperity and abundance, let's begin to imagine it can be ours. Bring that light in. Allow it to emanate and grow. Feel the light waves flow like ripples in the endless water. Imagine the light waves flowing outside of your body, outside of that small space in which you live, outside of the home, the block, the neighborhood, the greater community. Imagine the light waves rippling further even than the community, to the state, across the country, rippling across the oceans throughout the world, beyond our world into the universe, and beyond the universe to become one with the greatest source. The greatest universal light source of energy that is. That light is prosperous abundance, it is currency in flow. Allow yourself to float there comfortably, peacefully, in total calm. Your body is floating, bobbing as if you are in the water weightless, safe, surrounded by this universal abundant light. It can be yours, it is yours.

What do you see? What do you feel? Are you floating among silver coins jingling underneath you? Are you lying on green bills softly cushioned around you? There is light in that prosperous abundance, it can be yours, it is yours. Imagine the money-fading out to light, and fading back in to money, and fading back out to light. It is one and the same. Prosperous abundance is light in the form of love. Invite this love in as self-love. You are worthy, no matter what, no matter what.

Breathe in the love, it can be yours, it is yours. This love and light and prosperous abundance can be yours, it is yours. You can have it, it can be with you in every moment. Every moment that you think, 'There is enough.' 'I am enough.' This is self-energy.

Take a deep breath, breathe in the light and love and prosperity. 'There is enough.' 'I am enough.'

Let's return now. Back from the universe, back through the world, back across the oceans, back across the country, back through our community, our neighborhood, our street, our home, into the body.

You are back in your body, connected in love, to the universal source, with self-energy. You are safe. Take a moment and think to yourself, 'I am safe.' 'I am love.' 'I am prosperous abundance.' 'It can be mine.' 'It is mine.' *This* is self-energy.

Breathe now and breathe again. Feel your body connected to the ground through your feet, tap your toes on the ground, to feel grounded and centered. You are now centered and connected to prosperity; the currency, the light and love that is enough. When you are ready, open your eyes, welcome to your new world of prosperous abundance. It is yours. There is enough.

reflections

ON FLOWING MILK

You are a new mother! Feeding your child the milk from your breast, the Miracle of Life, may be natural but is not always easy. This meditation will help you relax into the life force that you offer your child.

Power. Control. Clarity. Confidence. We see it and envy it in others. How often do we feel it in ourselves?

Take a moment to breathe. Try to clear your mind. Take a breath now; deep breath in and long breath out.

It may be difficult, there may be distraction, there may be pain; surely there's the agony of burden. Of a new life, totally dependent, on you, on your life.

Breathe again, keep trying to clear your mind. Deep breath in and long breath out.

As you breathe now, imagine the systems in your body moving, flowing ....in with your breath, out with your breath. Blood flows throughout your body; energy, too, flows through your meridians. Every breath is a miracle, every flow a blessing. It is through this flow that your baby was conceived, grew in your womb and came out into the world. Breathe in, breathe out; breathe in, breathe out; systems flowing.

God made our bodies perfect. While in the womb, your baby's every need was filled. Total peace, total harmony, total nutrition, perfect silence, enough space. G-d made our bodies perfect.

We have exactly what is needed to continue to nourish our baby, now, here in the world with us in body, mind, and spirit. The milk created in our breasts is manna, the substance miraculously supplied as food to our ancestors in the wilderness. The world is like a wilderness to your baby, no? The milk in you screams to be poured down from the heavens, into your baby's mouth, nourishing, nurturing, flowing like the endless and everlasting tides of the sea.

See the flowing tides, wave upon wave. See your milk letting down, flowing easily through the miraculous cup G-d created; the perfect body. While still human, we have falls, scrapes, mishaps...even our miraculous pathways may get blocked occasionally... but still it's perfect; there will be healing, and there will be flow.

Every breath is a miracle, every flow a blessing.

As you hold your baby, look into the eyes of your future, of the future of our people. Your milk nourishes and nurtures that single future, and that future for all generations. It is your turn, your place to sit with this precious gift of life in you, flowing from one to the other. Imagine the flow, know it is there.

Breathe now, deep breath in and long breath out. And breathe again.

When you're ready, open your eyes; look around and ground yourself in the loving surroundings you've created for your baby and for all future generations. Let it flow.

notes

8

A JOURNEY OF LOVING & CLEANSING YOUR BODY

We are given one body in this life. While we live in a time where certain parts can be replaced, the overall body is a miracle that we want to honor, respect and support. This meditation can serve for illness or a deep desire for your best body.

Take a moment to breathe. Breathe in, breathe out. Begin to clear your mind. Breathe again. Create an opening in your mind for quiet, for peace.

Come to consciousness about the blessing of your body. Without fail, your body is strong, it carries you through your day. Each part of your body has purpose, each part supports you. Breathe now and think a grateful thought about your body.

Take this moment to do a mental scan.

Start at your toes, the extension of your feet that offers balance; without them you wouldn't be walking upright. Ten small digits, without which you would be off balance. When you are feeling ungrounded about anything in life, close your eyes for a second, breathe and focus on your toes. Bend your knees a little and feel the security of your feet on the ground.

Mentally scan your feet. They are the footing of your life, from your first step to the last step you took today, your feet have carried you. Breathe now and think a grateful thought about your feet.

Mentally scan up your strong legs, to your hips. Your hips are the foundation of your body. They hold the organs that allow you to become a mother. Honor your hips and all the organs and systems they hold up. Think about the strong and solid lower half of your body, think about the blood and energy rushing soundlessly, flowing smoothly. Breathe now and think a grateful thought about your foundation.

Scan up now through your mid-section. The mid-section of your body holds all of your organs. Spend some time with these precious parts that give you life-your heart, kidney, liver, spleen and lung. You may not understand what each organ is or does, but it's important to know-deep down-that each organ plays a

Come to consciousness about the blessing of your body.

role in the healthy functioning of your body.

Think of a complex and interconnected highway system- picture the cars whizzing by, cars in unison rushing along, coming from someplace and going to someplace. This is how you can actually see the blood and energy flowing easily throughout your body. There are pathways from organ to organ, can you see them? Picture these pathways now, clearly in a healthy flow. Imagine the organs as pit stops along the way, a carwash if you will; every stop clearing out, cleaning, scrubbing and leaving behind squeaky clean healthy living organs. Breathe now and think a grateful thought about your organs.

Continue up your body, now, to your upper back, shoulders and neck. Straighten your back now-picture the muscles up and down your entire back, strong and supportive. Bring your shoulders back and down and stretch your back. Feel the stretch and know this brings your body strength. Strength to support your midsection that cushions your organs, strength to walk upright for the rest of your life. Feel the difference in your mind, body and soul when you sit or stand straight, not with your shoulders and back hunched over as you are most of the time. Breathe now and think a grateful thought about your strong back that supports your upright body.

Move up your neck to your head, the head that holds your brain; there are literally billions of nerve cells and trillions of connectors there. Imagine the stars in the galaxy, endless, infinite. This is the power of your brain, if you know it, see it, feel it, feed it and protect it. Your brain gives meaning to the things that happen in you and around you, it controls thoughts and memory and speech and movement. Your brain controls your thoughts. You control your brain. You have the power to control your thoughts. When you think worried or uncomfortable thoughts about your body-inside or out- use the power of your brain to reframe these negative thoughts into loving and positive thoughts. Breathe now and think a grateful thought about your brain.

Breathe again. Deep breath in and long breath out.

Slowly scan down the body all the way back to your toes. It is now clean and strong and lovingly supports you every second that you are alive. You can do this scan at any moment; you do not need to be in a deep meditative space. Use the power of your thoughts to do a scan any time your thoughts turn to fear or worry or concern about your body. If you bring G-d into your thoughts with you, you will feel infinite love and support, always.

Breathe again, and put your hands over your heart and think one last grateful thought about your clean and strong body. When you're ready, open your eyes and look around you, look out a window if you can. Wiggle your toes and feel your balance.

reflections

9

FINDING YOUR INNER STRENGTH

What is that in you? Do you feel it, do you sense it? There is inner strength that lies in wait for you to find and to feel. This meditation will help you uncover it and share it with others.

Close your eyes now. Gently. take a deep breath in and let a long breath out. And again, take a deep breath in and let a long breath out. Begin to clear your mind. If there is too much going on there, just think the word 'clear' to yourself over and over. Picture an opening, a light space in the busy matter of your mind.

Now, imagine the brilliant summer sun, warm on your face, shining its bright rays into the space in your mind; illuminating the deep thoughts that are buried there.

What do you see? What are the thoughts you see

when the shining light hits them just right?

Do you have a deep desire about something that you want to do, to accomplish? Do you have a special quiet pride of something you know feels right to you?

Can you identify the special strengths that you have inside you, just sitting there waiting for that bright light to shine on them and bring them from seed to sprout?

It's helpful to take time to get quiet inside and feel and hear what your inner self wants you to know. Listen intently for any word or thought or idea that springs from this warm, comfortable sunny place. Allow your thoughts to just flow, let the sun continue to shine brightly as these thoughts hover and become tangible-from essence to root.

If you don't 'feel' anything happening, you can think about love. Think about a loving feeling you have for a family member, for your pet, for a friend. Think about love. What it feels like to be loved by others-to receive love; what it feels like to give love. If you did find other thoughts, combine those thoughts with the feeling of love you get from someone you love the most.

Breathe again, deep breath in and long breath out.

We are going to add a feeling of strength now to

This is a secret and special gift that you and only you have.

your inner thoughts, and to your thoughts of love.

Think of the sun filling you with strong light, with strength of thought....filling, filling until you feel full up and overflowing with these thoughts and love and strength. This is your inner strength. This is a secret and special gift that you and only you have. Only you have this inner strength; it's yours to return to and use whenever you want, whenever you need, or just whenever you feel like.

It is a blessing to share your light and your inner strength with others. You can do this by speaking with someone and connecting deeply with them, or you can do this simply in your own mind by offering love and strength to those around you. This is a precious gift that is yours, to share whenever you want. Share it often; sprinkle it around liberally. Most people yearn for love, they yearn for strength and they only dream of light. You have it to keep and hold onto for yourself, and you have it to give and to offer others support in any way they might need.

Now, breathe again, and begin to let the sun and the light recede. Deep breath in and long breath out. Begin to focus your mind back on your space, the here, the now. The brightness from the sun is now gone, but you can still feel the warmth-you can always feel the warmth whenever you want it. As you come back to the present, just know that you can share this light and warmth and strength with anyone around you. It's not a responsibility, but rather an opportunity; yours if you want it.

Open your eyes now, look around and get grounded in your space. You can find your inner strength whenever you need it.

reflections

10

WHAT DO I KNOW?

*This is a meditation to build your self confidence about what you do know. Find your point of self assurance and confidence in your **Knowing**.*

What do I know?

What do I really know?

What can I know for sure?

Take a moment to breathe now, deep breath in and long breath out.

Close your eyes, and breathe again. Let's explore together, the depths of self.

Feel your body first, do a scan now, from your toes to your crown. Feel yourself sitting, feel your core supporting you, your back straight, your shoulders comfortably down; feel yourself relax.

What does it take for my soul to shine?

Breathe again, in, and out.

Let's explore together, the depths of self; that which we *can* know.

What does it take for my soul to shine? It takes confidence, it takes calm. But where do I find them, they elude me.

Often, I am in pain. I am in physical pain for not having tended to my best health, to my body, to my nutrition, to rest, to hydration, to exercise.

Often, I am in confusion for not having tended to my mind. I spend too much time on electronics and neglect myself or others; I don't read, I don't discuss lofty or spiritual thoughts, I simply exist or respond to that which is around me.

Often, I am in depression for not having tended to my soul. I ignore nature's beauty, rain and resulting rainbows. I ignore God's creatures and the miracle of their existence. I ignore my imagination and the creative outlet it can offer me. I ignore song and the passion it can evoke in my heart. I ignore giving to others and the resulting justice that supports our world.

So where do I find confidence, calm and how do I connect to my soul's yearning to breathe freely, to live joyfully and to celebrate God's love, and to know?

The answer is to explore the depths of yourself. Make time to take mindful breaths; appreciate your lungs. Make time to ask yourself and others thought-provoking questions, connect intellectually and stimulate your brain. Make time to sing and dance, to paint and play; activate your soul. Your soul yearns to be seen, felt, to connect, to be touched, to be known.

This, then, will help you to know. To know yourself *and* to know that others may not be as they seem. Don't assume you know them. Just love them as they are, for who they are, however they are. Let's take a lesson from God, does He not love us exactly as we are? What if we are distracted from prayer, does He not still love us? What if we neglect the miraculous body He gave us, does He not still love us? What if we have caused pain? Does He not still love us?

And what of the person who caused you pain? What do you know? What do you really know? Might there be pain or confusion or depression in that person? Imagine that he or she is simply doing the best they can, as do we, day in and day out.

What do I know?

What do I really know?

What do I know for sure?

Take a moment now to consider; and when you're ready, breathe again and open your eyes. Feel your feet solidly grounded on the floor and breathe through the blessing of this foundation.

reflections

11

TOO MUCH

Life can feel overwhelming, so much going on around us, it is hard to find personal control. This meditation reminds you of the 'too much' syndrome that you may find grips you in its grasp. It reminds us that using our breath gives us the control back and can bring peace within.

Too much, too much, too much. Take a breath to ease your mind, deep breath in and long breath out. And again, deep breath in and long breath out.

Too much, too much, too much. For just this moment, ease your mind from the overwhelm of the day, the week, the world. You have it in you to do this right now, here and now. Yes, you do! Just start with your breath. Deep breath in and long breath out. And become aware of your thoughts, what are you thinking now, in this moment? Too many thoughts? Is it all just too much?

Use your own body to ground you. To come to center, just for this moment. Make yourself smaller, for just this moment it is okay to be small, not to be big, not to be brave, not to be fierce, not to aspire, and not to achieve. Just be small, in ease, in this moment.

Use your body to ground you. Start with your toes, feel them on the ground steady, solid, simply there. No pressure, no weight, just your feet on the ground, steady, solid, simply there.

Scan up to your legs, your knees, your hips, the center of your body that is solid and strong; no matter how it looks, no matter how it feels, it is your core, solid and strong. Scan up further now, your chest, your shoulders square but comfortable, your neck straight but limber, your head, your eyes, your crown, open and ready to receive the energy that serves you In This Moment. You are small now, in your body only, everything else is away. Not in you, not on your mind, not on your heart, not connected to your soul, you are free.

In this place you can now expand. Take a big breath in and hold 2,3 and let it out, long breath out 2, 3, 4. Feel the expansion of your chest and your innards; big breath in and long breath out. Expansion, but not overwhelm. It is not too much, it is not too much, it is not too much. You are enough to absorb that which is around you, you are enough. You are now expanded,

In this place you can now expand.

your energy glowing, Shining, flowing out in ripples vibrating around you. Ripples vibrating out to the world to help others who are feeling too much.

In this space we find the control we seek to simply be enough in this moment, and the next and the next. To be enough, you are enough. You feel easier now, in this moment. And your ease ripples out in vibrations around you, flowing out to the world to support others who are in 'too much.'

Let's come back to center now with a deep breath in and a long breath out, back to center, here and now. Scan back down through your core, down through your legs, down to your feet, and out through your toes, feel the ground solid and steady beneath your feet. You are grounded now, solidly grounded, you are enough.

reflections

B.O.A.T. MEDITATION TO FIND THE CALM WITHIN

*My life was changed when I learned how to 'open' and 'allow.' Then, on our sailboat one day, I conceptualized this four-step process. I was surprised at how it served me. The secret is in the **allowing**; not blocking that which is available to us if we simply breathe and open.*

Visualize yourself on a quiet boat on the calm water, gently rocking, rocking, rocking; everything around you is still and quiet. The universe around you is quiet, the gentle waves stir the soul.

Take a breath in 1,2,3, hold it for 1,2,3 and breathe out, 5,4,3,2,1.

And again in 1,2,3; hold 1,2,3 and breathe out 5,4,3,2,1.

In this breathing pattern, you are opening a pathway of light and love and clarity, a pathway for your soul to travel, for your soul to connect. Allow yourself to feel it, you are connecting to universal source, allow yourself to feel the warm light, it feels certain, clear and calm.

Take another quiet breath. **B**reathe-pause, **O**pen-pause, **A**llow-pause, **T**hink-pause.

In the clear quiet space that you create, insert the thoughts you choose: 'I am ok.' 'I am enough.' 'I'm in control.' 'I help uplift others.' 'I use my skills and energy to make a difference.' 'I have enough love for everyone.' 'I feel fulfilled.' 'I am on purpose.' Any thoughts you choose that fill your mind with good or best feeling, intention and desire. These thoughts feed your soul, and when your soul is sated, you are connected. Allow yourself the gift of self-loving thoughts. Your love will emanate out and spiral around others like a silk ribbon flowing and dancing in the air. You hold the end of that ribbon in your hand, you are loving kinetic energy, easily flowing gracefully in the orbit around you. Your soul dances on the other end, you and your soul are connected by that silky smooth strong ribbon.

Breathe again 1,2,3; hold 1,2,3 and breathe out 5,4,3,2,1. Open the clear and calm pathways, Allow the peace to fill you and think the thoughts that serve your best self, your soul-self; when we are our best, others

Allow yourself the gift of self-loving thoughts.

around us can be, too. When we are soul-connected, others around us rise.

Now, feel yourself back in the boat, feel the gentle rocking, feel the serenity. Take another quiet breath and when you're ready, open your eyes and know, the power is in you.

reflections

I HELP HEAL

Can anyone be a healer? Yes, if you know yourself, if you know your light, if you know your power to help. This meditation is to affirm your healing power to help others as we want to do.

I know my light. I help heal.

Take a deep breath in now, and a long breath out. And another.

I sit here in total calm, comfortable, with a full and certain knowing of my place in the world.

Take another deep breath in now, and long breath out.

Who am I? What am I intended to do here? I know that I am small, a speck in the great universe, a mite in the spectrum of all time. Yet I have learned that at any moment I might be the entire universe, the entire spectrum of time for one other who is in pain.

I know pain. And I can feel it in others deeply. emotional or physical. They hurt, and I hurt for them. But I know, I can help them heal. In ways big or small, mundane or profound; I listen, I feel, I share.

Pain lives in me, I face it; I love myself through it; I look for its source. I've learned its purpose, though I didn't plan for it, it helps me help others heal through pain.

Take another breath now, deep breath in and long breath out. I know my purpose, I feel God's light, His gift to me of my divine skill. But...Why? Could I not help without having experienced? Could I not love others deeply through their difficulties, still, without having felt? I wonder, I ask. I know it's ok.

Dear One, breathe through your questions, and accept the answers. Accept your special gift, the light-work of gently and compassionately helping others through their own experience.

Sit in your calm, comfortable space, with a full and certain knowing of your place in the world.

Breathe again, now, deep breath in and long breath out.

Know your light. You help heal.

reflections

14

ON COMPARISON

Comparing ourselves to others is one of the most destructive self-tendencies we have. Yet, is it not ingrained from our own childhood? Is it not part of the societal structure in which we live? This meditation encourages you to become aware of how you do this to yourself and suggests that you are enough just as you are now.

Why can't I be like her? Why does he seem to have it all? How did they do that, how did they get that?

Comparing ourselves to others is one of the gravest forms of self-detriment. Do you do this? Do you look around, sometimes, and wonder why other people seem to be succeeding, achieving, excelling and you're not?

Take a breath now, deep breath in, and long breath out. Let's clear our minds and open our hearts to the possibility that you could be enough. Just as you are; enough. Take another breath now, deep breath in and

Just as you are; enough.

long breath out.

Why is it that we compare ourselves to others? It is something that starts when we are young, younger than you even realize. New parents start feeling these feelings the minute a baby is brought home. Am I doing it right, getting it right? Am I doing it as well as others? Is this good enough, am I good enough? These are the thoughts and feelings that swirl around you as an infant. How could they not? There are no effective manuals for parenting. Books, teachers, classes - yes. But none of them exactly right for you. You are as individual as the stars. Your parents knew that you were unique, surely! But they did not realize that they were unique, too; uniquely qualified to be exactly your parents. Instead, the doubts and insecurities flooded them throughout your first days, weeks, months and possibly even your first few years.

This, then, surrounded you as you grew into the human you would become. Then, you entered society and school and life. All filled with people judging you because it was too hard for them to go in and see themselves.

Now, as the mature unique human you are, you have the opportunity to realize how much you compare yourself to others. It may be fully conscious for you, it may be subtle or even latent, but if you think, if you dig down deep now, you might see that you compare yourself to others.

Take a moment now to breathe, deep breath in and long breath out. Clear your mind and open your heart to your own self. To your uniqueness, your individuality, and the blessing and privilege of being alive. Why compare? Why is it that you, simply as you, cannot be good enough, cannot be enough?

Imagine the possibility of feeling that you are! Imagine what it would feel like to take a clear breath in and know that you are enough, you are good enough exactly as you are. Does this mean you stopped growing? No! We navigate the path of life forever, as long as we are in our physical body. We never stop growing, every moment is an opportunity to learn, to grow, to renew, to refresh the way you see yourself.

You are good enough. You are enough. You have all that you need to achieve, succeed, and excel in the way that you want. How? Start with your breath. Take a breath now, deep breath in, hold, hold, hold and long breath out. Clear your mind of the clutter that floods with thoughts of comparison. Look, seek, find the light, the clarity that you are enough exactly as you are. Doing the best you can is good enough. As you contemplate and reflect on who you are and on being enough, your soul will rise and feel better, and better, and better. You will feel lighter and airier. Now, as you breathe in and breathe out you can feel a lightness of being, a sense of self, a sense that you are enough.

Is it a sin to want more? No, it's wonderful! Never stop wanting, never stop striving, never stop aspiring to be the best you can be. But only in comparison to what you want, to who you are. Not because you think that is what you should do or because you feel that is what someone else wants.

Living a calm and confident life, feeling sure that you are on the path, on your way to exactly where you want to be—this does take dreams, imagine your success! What does that look like, what do you see, how does it feel? Go ahead and think about it! There's no harm in thinking and dreaming. The only harm is in not loving yourself and thinking that if you haven't yet achieved, then you aren't enough.

The more you breathe and clear, breathe and clear and the more you think and dream, and think and dream, the more your soul will find a place of comfort and be able to move in that direction, to help you accomplish exactly what you want. One step by one step. One step by one step. If you are able to move quickly in leaps and bounds, go ahead! But if that thought creates difficulty, concern, anxiety or fear then give yourself a break, do your soul a favor and take just one step. One step by one step by one step. Move forward in the direction of your dreams and before you know it, you *will* be enough. Then when others ask you how did you do that? Share the magic with them. Breathe and clear, think and reflect, journal and share, one step by one step by one step. Tell them, do not compare yourself to others, just be yourself, here and now, you are enough.

reflections

15

IN HEALING FOR ALL WHO HAVE SAID "ME, TOO"

This meditation is for anyone who was victimized. The child within suffers still. This meditation offers your adult self the opportunity to soothe that hurt child, to meld the healthy adult heart with the hurting child heart.

I want to heal, but I don't know how. Will I ever be normal again? What should I do, what should I do, what should I do? Should I name his name? [How will that serve?]

Was it my fault? Did I provoke, as he said I did, with my clothes, my beautiful hair, my growing breasts? Oh God, what can I do, what can I do, what can I do? Dear God and the universal source of all that is: please help me. I don't know what to do.

My Child, take a breath now, deep breath in and

It is all you.

long breath out. And again, deep breath in and long breath out.

You are here, now, in this moment, not 'that' moment. You are safe. Say the words to yourself, "I am ok. I am safe. Here and Now. In this moment, I am safe."

Turning towards the chill, the fear, the evil may haunt you. But can it help you? Only you know the answer. It is not necessary to look it in the face and relive the pain, the agony. It is only necessary to go in, go deep, find the child who is suffering. See her. Put your warm, loving, compassionate arms around the child. Just be quiet together until she stops shaking. This may take many tries, or it may take only once. Can you feel the safe warmth? Can you feel the intensity of love encircling you? The souls will meld, in safety, in warmth, in love. Breathe now, go deeper.

Go to the before time. Before, when you were free. Before, when you were whole. Before, when you were happy, innocent. Can you see her? Can you feel her spirit? Take the arms of the hurting one and put them around the happy one. Breathe. Can you feel the happy one encircling you with her arms of joy, of innocence, of love?

Can the happy one, the one who is free from pain, can she heal the other from the pain? You are she. You are the pain. You are the joy. You are the wise. You are the now. It is all you. Breathe now. Go deeper.

Do a body scan, start with the ground beneath your feet, the profound spirit of Mother Earth supporting you. Go up, feel your feet, feel your strong legs supporting you, feel your hips, your womanhood -it is beautiful and safe; feel your core-strong, straight-feel your heart, square your shoulders, loosen your neck, stand tall, feel proud. Now, allow the energy, the ball of fire that has been building to shoot up through your crown, up and out towards the sky, out into the new world that is now yours. The world is yours. It is not his.

Breathe again, now. Come back. Feel your feet grounded on the earth below, open your eyes, look out a window to see that the earth still turns. You are free. Breathe again. Turn your lips up in a knowing smile. Control is yours. Let fear and hatred go.

reflections

16

STAY ON THE PATH

When you wonder if you are going in the right direction for your life, this meditation offers the opportunity to take a breath, breakthrough your fear, keep your eyes in front of you and stay your course.

Stay on the path, stay on the path, stay on the path.

Take a deep breath in, hold it, then let a long breath out. And another, deep breath in and long breath out. Feel your mind clearing and opening to create a clear pathway to your success. Breathe again, hold, and let it out.

Everything that I have done has brought me to this path I am on today.

Stay on the path, stay on the path, stay on the path.

The trials and errors, the failures and successes, each one has brought me to this path that I am on. Stay

Does it feel right?

on the path, stay on the path, stay on the path.

Give yourself permission to focus on this path, now, breathe in, stretch out, and feel your heart opening to this path you are on. Stay on the path, stay on the path, stay on the path.

It may be narrow, it may be wide, it may be bumpy or smooth, but every step you have taken has lead you here, now. Stay on the path, stay on the path, stay on the path.

Give yourself permission to imagine what is ahead, right over the hill through which the path runs, what is that thing? What is that activity? Am I meant to go there? Then, breathe again and bring yourself back in and stay on the path, stay on the path, stay on the path.

It's ok to allow your mind to wander for a bit. What is your dream? What do you see, imagine the possibilities! Take a breath in, stretch out and feel your heart opening to reach your greatest success. Stay on the path, stay on the path, stay on the path.

Even while you imagine the worth, the benefits,

the beauty and goodwill that your big vision has, still it takes putting one foot in front of the other, on the path that you are on now. Stay on the path, stay on the path, stay on the path.

Take another breath in, and stretch out and feel your heart opening to the feeling 'it is right.' Does it feel right? If you feel discomfort, unease, then, by all means, take the next branch off the path where it veers, in a small new direction that is comfortable for you. One step after the other, then, stay on the path, stay on the path, stay on the path.

Permit yourself to know, to be sure, to feel certain. It's ok to try, it's good to fail so that you know that you can continue on. If you realize...there is no failure, there is no failure, there is no failure. There is only one step after the next, stay on the path, stay on the path, stay on the path.

Take another breath now, and stretch out and feel your heart open to the path ahead and while you look ahead, continue to put one foot in front of the other, calmly, surely, knowing *this path is yours*. Stay on the path, stay on the path, stay on the path.

Take a last breath now, stretch out and feel your heart opening to your success. The path is yours.

reflections

17

THERE IS LIGHT

Can you feel it? It feels like there is so much pain in the world. This meditation will help you move towards the light, towards the joy if you allow it. Take a break from the pain and look towards the light.

There is pain in the world tonight. Acknowledge this. Feel this. It's ok to feel sad for this; and yet, know, too that there is light.

Take a moment to breathe, deep breath in and long breath out. And breathe again, deep breath in and long breath out.

There is universal love, do you believe this? Take a moment now to think, do you believe in universal love? It is there, there in the light and warmth. There is a lightness of being in that Knowing.

Now, just for this moment, allow yourself to be free.

Free from the stress of the day.

Choose this feeling, in this moment.

Free from the difficulties in life.

Free from the negativity of others.

Free from the sadness in the world.

Free to be ok, just for the moment;

Free to allow yourself to move away from the sadness, from ok to good; and even from good to joy. Allow the source of universal love to provide the light and warmth, and know, just know that it can serve you. Choose this Knowing. Choose this feeling, in this moment.

And, if you choose, this is how you can feel now in this moment and in every moment; believing in universal love, in the light and warmth, now from that Knowing.

reflections

18

WHAT'S IT GOING TO TAKE?

"I wish..." "I want..." Do you have these thoughts, always wishing for something, always wanting more than you have? This meditation offers you the opportunity to figure out what it will take for you to grab the reigns and commit to life; make it happen the way you want.

I invite you to take a breath now, deep breath in and long breath out. While you take another breath, take a moment to clear your mind, to clear your thoughts, to open up your essence to allow the answer to this question: What's it going to take?

Take another breath in now, and release.

What's it going to take?

What's it going to take for you to live life as you want it to be? Will it take more money? Will it take more time? Will it take more material things? What's it going to take?

Imagine the possibility that the life you lead right now is exactly the life you want it to be. Clear your mind, imagine that thought. The life I lead right now is exactly as I want it to be.

Could it be? Is it possible? Imagine the possibility that you can wake up in the morning and start your day in a calm, comfortable, and happy way. Knowing that the day ahead can bring life exactly as you want it to be.

What is that life for you? What does it look like? What does it feel like? If you do not know the answer to these questions, you will never live life exactly as you want it to be. The idea will be forever elusive.

Do you realize what you do to yourself? Do you realize the thought that goes through your mind on a continuous loop, I wish, I wish, I want, I want..... something other than what I have now. Does that feel familiar to you?

Imagine the possibility that your life could be exactly as you want it to be. Take a moment to breathe now, come to awareness of what you do to yourself, in a continual Loop of I wish, I wish, I want, I want.

Come to clarity now, what is it that you want? What is it that you really want? Imagine the possibility that you could live life exactly as you want it to be, just calm, feeling okay, feeling on track, on purpose, even being happy with who you are, what you do and what

The life I lead right now is exactly as I want it to be. you have. The responsibility is yours, you can be okay with where you are and still desire and aspire to grow, to achieve, to move forward on your own path, on your own journey feeling good.

Let's take another breath now, clear mind, clear heart, soul-connected. Deep breath in and long breath out.

Imagine the possibility that you could live life exactly as you want it to be. What's it going to take?

reflections

CONCLUSION

Feeling Clear and Open, What's Next?

Dear friend,

I am simply delighted to be on the journey with you of self-reflection and self-discovery. I hope these meditations will be with you forever. I have learned of the beauty and power of repetition in my life and I want to assure you that repetition helps for the times that you lapse or regress. When meditations like these are fully integrated through repetition, you can call on them in service whenever needed.

My wish for you: *May these meditations become cataloged in your mind, available to you whenever needed for whatever mindful connection will serve your highest purpose.* Amen.

If you have been inspired to write your own meditations, wonderful! This shows spiritual unleashing the likes of which you might not have previously imagined but is now manifest from your own personal odyssey. I encourage you to write, there is room for all.

It is the greatest blessing to be able to take a clear breath, to quiet your mind, to relax your body and just be; just be. Take this blessing and go forth on your journey. Be aware that the journey shapeshifts as you ascend higher on to new plains of conscious awareness and descend deeper into new levels of inner quiet to soul-consciousness. As you go both higher and deeper you will breathe even more easily. It is the greatest gift of all, the miracle of a simple breath. With this book, I gift this miracle to you.

Please stay in touch.

With love,

Susan

WITH SUCH GRATITUDE

Do you believe it when people tell you something positive about you? Or, do you automatically tell yourself that it's 'not really true'? Do you find yourself doing that? This is what happened with my guided meditations. My dear friends said they loved them, but of course, I suspected they were 'not that good.' I thought my friends were just being supportive. Then, I used my own coaching Tool 'Reframe to Positive' [yes, I use my own Tools all the time!] and wondered, 'What if they mean it? What if my meditations are helpful? What if my words help just one person breathe a bit easier, clear and feel even just a bit better?' I breathed, got clear myself and leaped into the positive. I decided to believe them! This inspired me to write more, offer more and create the Virtual 20-Minute Zen-Retreat in which I share my guided meditation frequently with such positive feedback! And so, I offer such gratitude to my dearest friends, thank you for your constant love and support.

NOTE: If you are interested in bringing the Virtual 20-Minute Zen Retreat to your home or office, please contact me at susan@confident-life.com, or find information on my website at www.whatwillyourlegacybe.com.

ABOUT THE AUTHOR

Susan Axelrod, CCP, is the go-to Confidence Coach for Women. Specializing in working with executive women and matriarchs in mid-life who have spent decades doing for others... IT'S YOUR TURN NOW. What does 'my turn' look like? Using co-creative and co-facilitative coaching methods, Susan helps clients uncover the inspired soul within who is looking to live out the second half of life in a self-fulfilling and purposeful way. Susan doesn't give answers or advice. She works with clients to dig into their core, to explore the girl she was and the woman she wants to be for the rest of her life, personally, professionally, spiritually and physically. Using original Confident-Life™ Tools, Susan helps women find the Clarity and Confidence they seek to live out a Best Life. She works with women in transition who declare themselves 'READY!' ...ready to GROW, ready to LIVE now and create a meaningful and lasting legacy. Susan's contagious enthusiasm and deep listening skills spark and motivate clients to get Confident and Thrive!

Susan's Motivational Speaking and Confident-Life Workshops™ are a hit every time! Available for work-teams, book clubs, friend groups, women CEO clubs, nonprofits or any place women gather.

Certified Coach Practitioner, through The Coach Training Academy [accredited by the International Coaching Federation and Certified Coaches Alliance].

CONNECT WITH SUSAN

Imagine the Possibilities.

Are you ready to live a more Confident-Life™?

Contact Susan now, you'll be glad you did.

When you call, Susan responds.
Everything is timely, 100% personal and 100% custom.

Please learn about Susan and her work here:
www.whatwillyourlegacybe.com.

CONTACT:
susan@confident-life.com | 518-495-4573

TESTIMONIALS

"I promise anyone reading this testimonial that if you are experiencing some sort of challenge, Susan has a way of helping you create clarity in very simple & doable ways that bring about results!! Speaking from personal experience, she is a master at that!"
-Carlenia Springer, www.destinyembraced.com

"Thank you SO MUCH! In just that single call, I feel like a new woman! A more confident woman. You're definitely A Confidence Coach! Hugs!"
-Savana Rose Woods, Authenticity Marketing

"You are often in my thoughts and I derive a lot of pleasure from seeing all your accomplishments and all the energy you put into helping people better themselves. I could go on and on. Bottom line is that I know that were it not for our conversations a few years ago, I would not be who I am today and dealing with life in the way that I do now. I am so deeply grateful."
-Natasha Stephenson-Guttman

FREE AUDIO OF GUIDED MEDITATIONS IN THIS BOOK

As a thank you for buying this book, I am pleased to offer you a free audio bundle of the meditations, enjoy!

Find them here:
www.whatwillyourlegacybe.com/freeaudiomeditations

www.ingramcontent.com/pod-product-compliance
Lightning Source LLC
Chambersburg PA
CBHW071411290426
44108CB00014B/1775